D1520674

SPACE TO
EXPLORE

# The
# Psychedelic
# Journal

By Jamie C Johnstone
& Jon Waterlow

Cover and illustrations: Jamie C Johnstone

(www.jamiecjohnstone.com)

Poetry by JJ Bitters © 2020

ISBN 978-1-9993434-1-5

First published in London, 2020

We do not promote or endorse the use of substances which may be illegal where you are. We provide a list of additional resources where you can learn more about various psychedelic and other mind-altering substances. It's vital that you make yourself aware of the potential risks and hazards – personal, pharmacological and legal – before taking any psychedelic. Your choices remain your responsibility. *The Psychedelic Journal* is not a 'how to' book and is not offered with the intention of providing advice.

*Para el bien de todos*

*For the good of all*

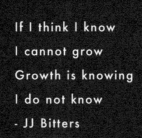

If I think I know

I cannot grow

Growth is knowing

I do not know

- JJ Bitters

# Space To Explore

Psychedelic experiences are as old as humanity itself. From the timeless shamanic traditions of Siberia and the Amazon to the vision quests of Native Americans, from the traces of cannabis discovered in Shakespeare's pipe to the psychedelic-inspired music of the Beatles or Pink Floyd, communities and individuals have always sought altered states of consciousness as a means to unlock their creativity, connect with their emotions, and to touch the transcendent.

Psychedelic experiences can be incredibly profound and yet all too fleeting. As we shift back into 'normality,' even major insights and personal breakthroughs can fade like a dream in the cold light of morning. This journal can be a place to preserve your experiences – somewhere to keep a note of what you found in those other realms, be it in the form of notes, poems, drawings, or anything else that carries meaning for you.

The idea behind this journal is to offer you 'Space to Explore.' We've aimed to provide only the lightest of structures so that you can make this journal your own. The pages before you can become whatever you want them to be: they might be a playground for your creativity, or perhaps they'll become a safe space in which to explore yourself more deeply.

There's no pressure to create 'Art' with a capital 'A' here. Simply drawing some lines, doodling, writing a single word or connecting some dots can be a great way to help your mind get free, playful and exploratory. Some pages in the journal don't make conventional sense: lines appear and disappear unexpectedly; images are warped or upside-down; empty spaces in which to write or draw are entangled with colour, landscapes and animals. This is all designed to encourage a childlike sense of wonder and play; how you interact with these elements is always entirely up to you.

There's space in the journal for 21 'trips,' with a prompt to write the date if you want to anchor them to a particular time. The idea is to create a record you can revisit, both to remind yourself of what you learnt and experienced, and to help you to see the often subtle changes that can emerge over time.

The invitation is to use this space to explore your experience, your perceptions, and your mind. Alongside the beautiful original artwork, we've brought together some quotations, poetry, and prompts to help inspire creativity, reflection and insight. The prompts are intentionally short and open-ended: they're a starting point, but the journey you take will always be distinctly your own.

Quite a few of the prompts originate in one way or another from Buddhism. We include these not to promote any particular view of the world or the self, but because Buddhism has specialised for millennia in inviting us to 'find out for ourselves.' Buddhism asks questions that prompt us to go looking for our own answers, rather than telling us what we ought to find there.

We hope that this journal will be a helpful and stimulating companion for you as you set out to explore what lies beyond the doors of perception.

Safe travels!

*The poetry in this journal is by the immensely talented JJ Bitters. You can find more of his work on Instagram @jj.bitters, Twitter @jj_bitters and at jointheunknown.com.*

SUGGESTIONS:

Art supplies (pens, pencils, paints, etc.)

Music playlist

Atmospheric lighting

Plants

Musical instruments

Tissues

Yoga mat

Bodywork tools you're familiar with using (e.g., foam roller)

Photographs of things/people which are meaningful to you

Picture books

Poetry books or recordings

Incense

Meaningful objects

# Before You Begin

Psychedelic experiences are powerful and not to be taken lightly. Many people put a great deal of thought into preparing for their journey, cultivating a calm and focused mindset, and making sure their environment is both safe and stimulating.

We've compiled a few suggestions below to help you design the perfect launch-pad for your journey.

ESSENTIALS:

Water

Sensitive scales

Comfortable clothing

A basin or bucket in case you feel sick

Some snacks

Blanket and pillow

Phone on Do Not Disturb

*The Psychedelic Journal*

Psychedelic experiences are often profound and yet strangely ephemeral. They can radically change our perceptions of self, space, time and everything in between; and yet, unless we apply conscious attention and reflection, they often fade over time. We've created this journal as a space in which to play and explore, but also to serve as an effective tool to support integration and personal growth.

We suggest expanding each psychedelic experience, both so that you're mentally and emotionally prepared beforehand, and to create space to reflect and integrate what you learned and experienced afterwards.
To do so, consider following these simple steps to help get the most out of this journal and your psychedelic journeys:

## Five Days Before Your Trip:

- Take out this journal and choose a prompt you want to reflect on

- What intention do you have for this trip? Make a note of this

- Read through some of your previous entries to remind yourself of recurring themes and persistent questions


## Five Days After Your Trip:

- Read over your last entry. What stands out to you? Is there an overarching theme or emotion? How do you feel about it now?

- Ask yourself some future-oriented questions: Are there changes you want to make in your life and behaviour? What would you do differently next time?

- Add some notes now that you've had time to reflect – and continue to revisit them regularly to see if and how you're integrating what you've learned

# Additional Resources

A Psychedelic Renaissance has been gathering momentum for more than 20 years. Scientists have taken up the torch abandoned in the tense political climate of the 1960s and are demonstrating with academic rigour that mind-altering substances hold immense power to heal psychological wounds and can help people to construct lives they find meaningful.

There are many fantastic resources out there, some of them freely available online, which you can investigate to learn more about this fascinating field and its history.

## History of Psychedelic Culture and Research

Michael Pollan, *How to Change Your Mind: The New Science of Psychedelics* (London, 2018).

David Nutt, *Drugs – Without the Hot Air: Minimising the Harms of Legal and Illegal Drugs* (Cambridge, 2012).

Ben Sessa, *The Psychedelic Renaissance: Reassessing the Role of Psychedelic Drugs in 21st Century Psychiatry and Society* (London, 2012).

# Information, Interviews and Research

**Erowid:** *erowid.org*

> A classic online resource that provides reliable, non-judgemental information about psychoactive plants, chemicals, and related issues.

**Imperial College London Centre for Psychedelic Research:**
*imperial.ac.uk/psychedelic-research-centre*

> Led by Dr Robin Carhart-Harris, this academic research centre regularly publishes groundbreaking research into the potential uses of psychedelics to treat depression and other mental health conditions. They also use psychedelics as tools to probe the brain's basis of consciousness.

**Johns Hopkins Center for Psychedelic & Consciousness Research:**
*hopkinspsychedelic.org*

> An academic hub of pioneering psychedelics research, the Johns Hopkins Center studies how psychedelics affect behaviour, mood, cognition, brain function, and biological markers of health.

**Multidisciplinary Association for Psychedelic Studies (MAPS):**
*maps.org*

> Founded by Dr Rick Doblin in 1986, MAPS is a non-profit research and educational organisation at the forefront of psychedelic research. Its rigorous, scientific approach has brought psychedelic-assisted therapy a step closer to legalisation in the United States.

**Psychedelics Today:** *psychedelicstoday.com*

An educational website and podcast exploring important research into psychedelics and non-ordinary states of consciousness. Psychedelics Today also provides in-depth courses such as 'Navigating Psychedelics,' focusing on safety, self-care, and the importance and complexity of integrating the insights of psychedelic experiences into everyday life.

**The Third Wave:** *thethirdwave.co*

This website provides useful and accessible information about numerous mind-altering substances. They are particularly interested in, and sell a course on, micro-dosing.

## Psychedelic Retreats

**Synthesis:** *synthesisretreat.com*

Synthesis offers safe, legal, medically supervised psychedelic retreats in Amsterdam. They make the psychedelic experience accessible to curious individuals who want to utilise moderate-to-high doses of psilocybin truffles to catalyse creative breakthroughs, explore consciousness, find meaning, improve confidence, and search for a mystical experience.

**The Psychedelic Society:** *psychedelicsociety.org.uk*

In addition to its wide-ranging programme of events (from meditation to bodywork, community-building to sound baths), The Psychedelic Society also runs regular, legal psychedelic retreats in The Netherlands.

**SpiritQuest Sanctuary:** *biopark.org*

A shamanic sanctuary located in the Amazon Rainforest in Peru, founded by Don Howard Lawler in 1995. SpiritQuest provides traditional healing retreats centred around plant medicines such as Ayahuasca and Huachuma (San Pedro), taken within a ceremonial context. From personal experience, we can say that SpiritQuest Sanctuary is an exceptionally safe and ethical centre at which retreats are conducted with the utmost integrity.

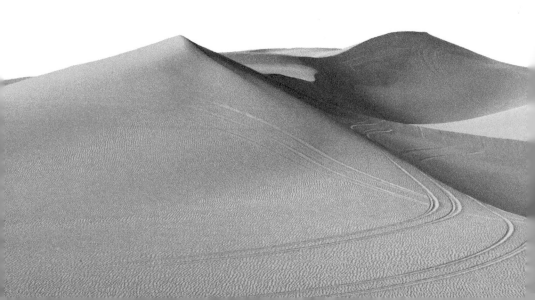

TIME TO
EXPLORE

'*FICTION
INVENTS
REALITY*'

- Terry Pratchett

How do you feel right now?                              /    /

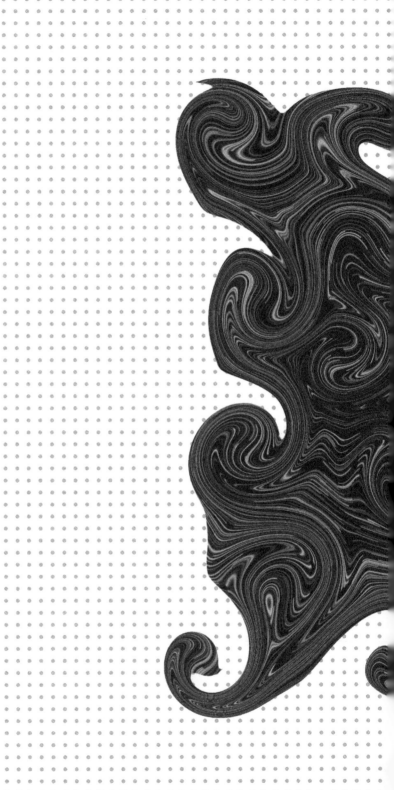

# What part of you does the world not see?

/ /

'THE INTUITIVE MIND IS A SACRED GIFT AND THE
RATIONAL MIND IS A FAITHFUL SERVANT. WE HAVE
CREATED A SOCIETY THAT HONOURS THE SERVANT
AND HAS FORGOTTEN THE GIFT'
- Albert Einstein

If clouds roll in

And paint a blue night grey

Remember

Clouds come and go

But the stars always stay

- JJ Bitters

*'MOMENT AFTER MOMENT, EVERYTHING COMES OUT FROM NOTHINGNESS. THIS IS THE TRUE JOY OF LIFE'*
- Shunryu Suzuki

What is real, right here and now?                    /    /

# What could I add to my life that excites me?

'*WHEN THERE IS JUDGEMENT PRESENT,*
*THERE'S ZERO SPACE FOR GROWTH*'
- Philip McKernan

If held down
I cannot grow
To be more
I must let go
- JJ Bitters

Who is reading these words? / /

*'HEART FORWARD AND HEAD UP'*

- Don Howard Lawler

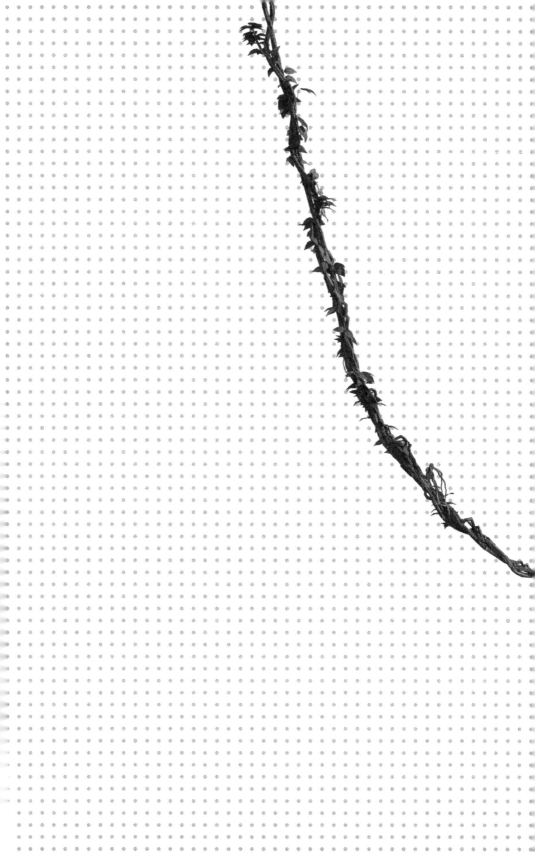

How does stretching or yoga feel right now?
Try exploring how your body is connected.

/ /

'WE SHOULD CONSIDER EVERY DAY LOST ON WHICH
WE HAVE NOT DANCED AT LEAST ONCE. AND WE
SHOULD CALL EVERY TRUTH FALSE WHICH WAS NOT
ACCOMPANIED BY AT LEAST ONE LAUGH'
- Friedrich Nietzsche

'IN THE BEGINNER'S MIND THERE ARE MANY
POSSIBILITIES,
BUT IN THE EXPERT'S THERE ARE FEW'
- Shunryu Suzuki

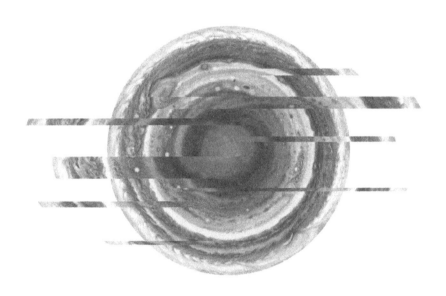

What would you like to learn?          /    /

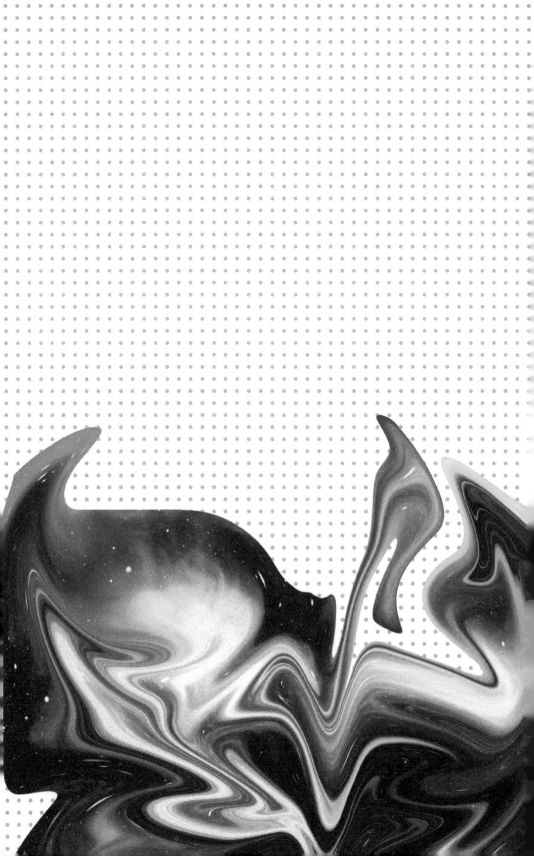

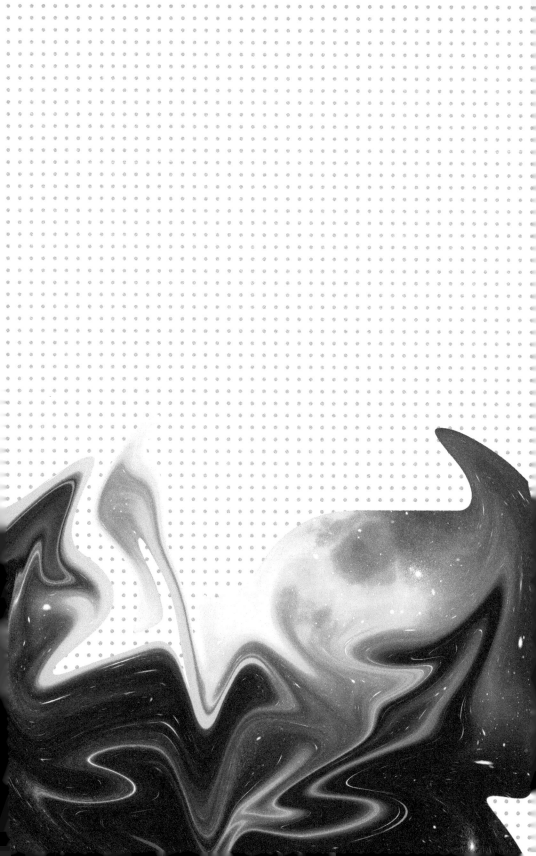

What are the 3 happiest moments in your life?  / /

*'LIFE LEAVES CLUES'*

- Philip McKernan

See ME

in WE

- JJ Bitters

*'YOU ARE THE SKY.
EVERYTHING ELSE
– IT'S JUST THE
WEATHER'*
- Pema Chödrön

What is reality?

What's hiding inside your secret heart?                    /    /

'FOR THINGS TO REVEAL THEMSELVES TO US, WE NEED TO BE READY TO ABANDON OUR VIEWS ABOUT THEM' – Thich Nhat Hanh

It seems that life is at its best
when I'm BEING more

and doing less
- JJ Bitters

'YOU'RE UNDER NO OBLIGATION TO BE THE SAME
PERSON YOU WERE FIVE MINUTES AGO'
- Alan Watts

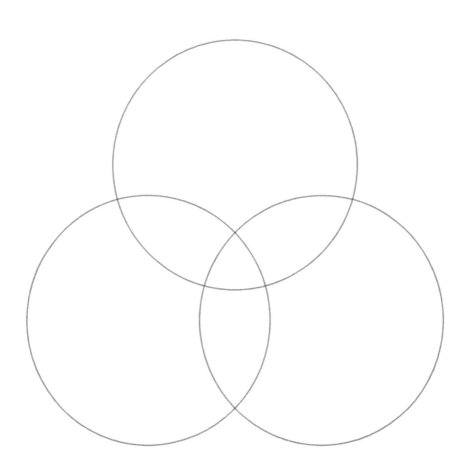

Where in your life are things in and out of balance?   /   /

How does your body feel?          /          /

'IT IS SAID THAT YOUR LIFE FLASHES BEFORE YOUR
EYES JUST BEFORE YOU DIE. THAT IS TRUE,
IT'S CALLED LIVING'
- Terry Pratchett

*'THE PRIVILEGE OF A LIFETIME IS BEING WHO YOU ARE'*

- Joseph Campbell

If you had unlimited resources,
how would you live your life?

/ /

'IF YOU CAN SOLVE THE PROBLEM, THEN WHAT IS
THE NEED OF WORRYING? IF YOU CANNOT SOLVE IT,
THEN WHAT IS THE USE OF WORRYING?'
- Shantideva

time is a wheel
spinning around
the Now is the axis
where time is bound
- JJ Bitters

*'THERE IS NO RUSH TO BEING'*

- Cory Allen

What was your favourite book or show as a child?
What did it teach you?

/ /

What does your perfect day look like?                    /    /

'*THE RAYS OF THE SUN DO INDEED TOUCH*
*THE EARTH, BUT STILL ABIDE AT THE SOURCE*
*FROM WHICH THEY ARE SENT*'
- Seneca

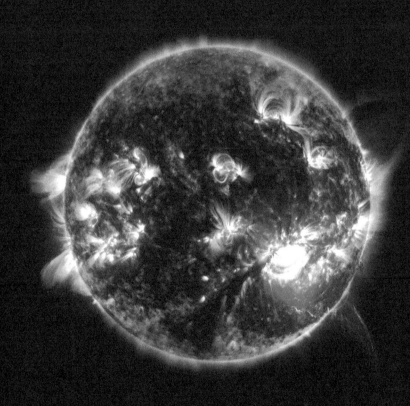

'SUCCESS IS MANUFACTURED IN THE MIND WHILE
HAPPINESS IS CULTIVATED IN THE SOUL'
- Philip McKernan

Do I love what I do? Do I want to do something else?        /        /

If you wrote a letter to your teenage self, what would you say? What would you want them to know?

*'THANK YOU,*
*I'M SORRY,*
*I LOVE YOU,*
*FORGIVE ME'*

- Ho'oponopono

*Traditional Hawaiian practice of*

*reconciliation and forgiveness*

'MUDDY WATER IS
BEST CLEARED BY
LEAVING IT ALONE'
- Alan Watts

What do you see right now?                    /    /

You're the surfer

Not the ocean

You can't control the tide

But if you practice balance

You can enjoy the ride

- JJ Bitters

What is a place you would like to return to?

/ /

*'COMING BACK TO WHERE YOU STARTED IS NOT THE SAME AS NEVER LEAVING'*

- Terry Pratchett

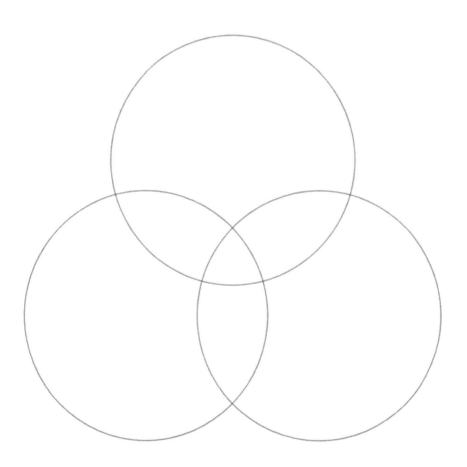

'ENLIGHTENMENT IS YOUR CURRENT REALITY WITHOUT THE STORIES.' - Cory Allen

How do other people see me? Why?                    /    /

With stillness & patience

Muddy waters clear

Mind being empty

The Now will appear

- JJ Bitters

THIS TOO
SHALL PASS

CPSIA information can be obtained
at www.ICGtesting.com
Printed in the USA
LVHW072006030423
743358LV00015B/802/J

9 781999 343415